WOMEN OF SPORTS

THE BEST OF THE BEST
in
Figure Skating

BY
RACHEL RUTLEDGE

M
THE MILLBROOK PRESS
BROOKFIELD, CONNECTICUT

Produced by
CRONOPIO PUBLISHING
John Sammis, President
and
TEAM STEWART, INC.

Series Design and Electronic Page Makeup by
JAFFE ENTERPRISES
Ron Jaffe

Researched and Edited by
Mark Stewart and Michael Kennedy

All photos courtesy
AP/WIDE WORLD PHOTOS, INC.
except the following:

BONGARTS PHOTOGRAPHY, SPORTSCHROME USA
Cover (Tara Lipinski winning the 1998 Olympic gold medal)

Printed in the United States of America

Published by
The Millbrook Press, Inc.
2 Old New Milford Road
Brookfield, Connecticut 06804

Library of Congress Cataloging-in-Publication Data

Rutledge, Rachel.
  The best of the best in figure skating/ by Rachel Rutledge.
  p.   cm.   —(Women of Sports)
  Includes index.
  Summary: Discusses the past and future of women's figure skating and presents biographies
of eight of the sport's most famous skaters: Oksana Baiul, Surya Bonaly, Nancy Kerrigan,
Michelle Kwan, Tara Lipinski, Chen Lu, Katarina Witt, and Kristi Yamaguchi.
  ISBN 0-7613-1302-8 (lib. bdg.).—ISBN 0-7613-0444-4 (pbk.)
  1. Women skaters—Biography—Juvenile literature.   2. Skating—Juvenile literature.
[1. Ice skaters. 2. Women—Biography. 3. Ice skating] I. Title.   II. Series: Best of the best in
figure skating.
GV850.A2R88 1998
796.91'2'0820922
[B]—DC21

                                                                                          98-25634
                                                                                             CIP
                                                                                              AC

                                      pbk: 10 9 8 7 6 5 4 3 2 1
                                      lib: 10 9 8 7 6 5 4 3 2 1

CONTENTS

In the Beginning

Many sports recognize athletes for artistry and grace, but only figure skating actually makes those qualities a major part of a competitor's score. Indeed, women figure skaters have been called "athletes in disguise." No one works as hard or practices as long as skaters, and few athletes can perform the precision acrobatics they do. Yet for as long as the sport has been around, the idea of "femininity" has been central to winning. This means more than looking pretty or having a great costume—it also translates into making the difficult look easy. Consequently, the best skaters are not even known for their strongest moves, except by those close to the sport.

How long has the sport existed? No one knows for sure. The answer probably depends on one's definition of what a sport is. It is known that people have been skating for a very long time. Early explorers of North America were amazed to see members of the Iroquois nation gliding across frozen lakes and rivers on blades fashioned of bone. This suggests that they had been skating for quite a while, as do the many ancient bone-and-shoe combinations that have been unearthed by archaeologists.

In Europe, skating dates back to the 1300s, when the first wooden skates were used as a means of transportation on Holland's frozen canals. The word "skates," in fact, comes from the Dutch word "schaats." Skating got a boost in popularity during the mid-17th century, when King Charles II of England returned home after a period of exile in Holland. While there, he had become very interested in skating. Soon England's wealthiest and most influential individuals were enjoying themselves on the ice. Others soon took up this pastime, and many enjoyed the challenge of trying to repeat a set pattern of turns (or "figures") again and again. Thus over the next 200 years, the "sport" of figure skating gradually evolved.

For young women anxious to get out and get some exercise during the winter, skating was an ideal choice. It provided a wonderful opportunity to tone the muscles and get some fresh air, and it gave women a chance to show how graceful they were. Some skated with men, some skated alone, and some formed clubs so they could skate with other women of similar age and social standing. The first organized competitions were held at "winter carnivals" in the early 1800s. Prizes were generally awarded to those who combined an interesting costume with good skating skills. In other words, looks counted for a lot, but not everything. Already, a definite tone was being set for the sport's future.

The big breakthrough in figure skating came from an American man named Jackson Haines. A popular dancer, Haines decided to try some of his moves on ice skates during a European tour in 1864. Soon, people on both sides of the Atlantic were skating to music. Often, bands would play at the edge of a lake while skaters twirled around the ice. This new artistic twist greatly increased the popularity of skating, and in 1891 the International Skating Union was formed. By the turn of the century, rules had been laid out to govern formal competitions, and skating became a true competitive sport.

In 1908, women's figure skating was included in the Olympics for the first time. The gold medal went to Madge Syers, a highly decorated competitor who came out of retirement and was the unanimous choice of all the judges. The sport reappeared at the 1920 Olympics in Antwerp, Belgium, and Sweden's Magda Julin won the gold. Julin's victory illustrates how strange and subjective figure skating can be. All but one of the judges voted for a woman from his or her country. Julin received no first-place votes, yet enough judges placed her second (perhaps believing she was not a threat to "their skater") that Julin ended up winning!

That figure skating was dominated by politics and intrigue eight decades ago comes as no surprise to those who know the sport today. In many ways, little has changed. The biggest difference? The quality of the skating and the look of the skaters. Prior to the 1920s, the top competitors were women wearing drab, ankle-length dresses, performing rather uninspired compulsory programs. It was very dull by today's standards. That all changed when an 11 year old sensation named Sonja Henie arrived at the 1924 Olympics.

Already the national champion of Norway, Henie idolized world-famous ballerina Anna Pavlova. She believed that skating should be more like ballet, with its athletic jumps and spins, and its dramatic appeal. She entered the skating competition in a knee-length dress and promptly finished last, because of the heavy penalties she drew with her jumps. The major skating associations frowned on women jumping, believing it was unsafe and unhealthy, and the judges were simply following the rules of the time. Henie, however, energized the crowd. No skater had ever drawn the wild applause she did, and no one had ever attracted so much attention to the sport. By the 1928 Olympics, jumping was not only allowed, it was practically required.

Henie, just 15, won her first of three gold medals in 1928. In 1930, her parents took her to America, outfitted her in a dazzling costume, and entered her in the World Championships at New York's Madison Square

Garden. She was an unprecedented sensation. America and the rest of the planet was completely in love with the precocious champion. Henie won the world title that year, and took eight more during the 1930s. In 1936, she turned professional and toured the U.S. in her own ice show. The country was in the depths of the Great Depression, but for Sonja fans packed one arena after another. Later, she signed a contract to make movies for 20th Century Fox. Her first film, "One in a Million," was a huge success, and for many years she ranked among Hollywood's top box office draws. Henie starred in 11 movies and took her Hollywood Ice Revue on the road for many years. During that

People could not get enough of Sonja Henie. She revolutionized her sport as a teenager, then went on to fame and fortune with her Hollywood Ice Revue in the 1930s.

time, millions of people bought ice skates. In the end, Henie not only transformed her sport—she created an entire new industry.

After World War II, Canada's Barbara Ann Scott distinguished herself as the world's best skater. She won the gold medal at the 1948 Winter Olympics in St. Moritz, Switzerland and became one of the most talked-about athletes in North America.

The next skater to win the hearts of the world was Canada's Barbara Ann Scott, who dominated skating after the second world war. In 1948, she won World, European, and Olympic gold medals and was hailed for her blend of femininity, artistry, and athletic talent. Almost overnight, figure skating became Canada's hottest sport, and the company that marketed the Barbara Ann Scott doll made millions. During the 1950s, America's Tenley Albright and Carol Heiss took home most of the major medals. Albright, who was trained by Maribel Vinson (the top U.S. skater during Sonja Henie's reign), overcame polio to become an Olympic and world champion. She was daring, original, and brought great intelligence to her performances. After her skating career she became a renowned surgeon. Heiss was every bit as successful as Albright, winning five World Championships and a gold medal at the 1960 Olympics. In a classic storybook wedding, she married Hayes Jenkins, the world's top male figure skater. She went on to become one of the country's most accomplished skating coaches.

In the mid-1950s, America's Tenley Albright ruled the figure skating world. She won the gold medal at the 1956 Olympics, edging out Carol Heiss.

A 1961 plane crash wiped out the U.S. skating team, but within a few years, the country was back on the map. In 1964, Peggy Fleming captured her first of five straight national titles, then began studying with Carlo Fassi, whom many regard as the sport's greatest teacher. Fleming had

A tragic plane crash devastated American figure skating during the 1960s. Peggy Fleming filled this void and emerged as a special champion.

something special. She was a shy young woman who seemed to "find herself" on the ice. She showed incredible emotion in her skating, and interpreted her music unlike anyone else in the sport. Fleming could also perform stunning moves. At the 1966 World Championships, she produced gasps when she unveiled a brand new combination: the double-axel/spread-eagle double-axel. At the 1968 Olympics, she so out-classed the competition that the gold medal was decided before the final programs were skated.

In 1976, Carlo Fassi produced another champion in Dorothy Hamill. She too had an appeal that seemed to transcend skating. Hamill was the "girl next door." She was small, nearsighted, and had a cute haircut that bounced and twirled as she did. She also happened to be a brilliant skater. There was no jump or spin Hamill could not perform, and

Dorothy Hamill captivated millions of little girls with her gold medal performance in the 1976 Olympics, and gave figure skating an important boost.

she responded to pressure like a champion. As Sonja Henie had done nearly 50 years earlier, Hamill touched off a skating revolution. She also had the most-copied haircut in the world for several years after winning the gold medal at the 1976 Olympics.

Thanks to superstars like Fleming and Hamill, the stakes in the sport got extremely high. Professional skaters could make as much money as women in other sports, particularly if they had "name recognition" from the Olympics.

The lengths to which some women would go to gain an edge became ludicrous. During the late-1970s, for instance, the two best skaters were Linda Fratianne and Anett Potzsch. Each had won a World Championship heading into the 1980 Olympics, and each was determined to win the gold. Believing themselves to be equals from a talent standpoint, they made drastic alterations to their bodies in hopes of gaining

How Skating is Scored

Figure skating competitions are broken into two programs. The short program lasts two minutes, during which a skater must distinguish herself from her rivals, particularly in the area of technical skill. Certain maneuvers are required of all competitors, and judges must deduct points if a skater fails to perform any of these elements properly. The short program counts for one-third of a skater's overall score.

The long program lasts four minutes, and is considered a "free skate." Here judges look for artistic interpretation, as well as the technical difficulty of a routine. If one of the top three finishers in the short program wins the long program, she automatically wins the event. For a skater finishing the short program lower than third, it takes big mistakes by those ahead of her to win. If two skaters tie in the short program, the winner is the one whose technique as the sharpest. If two skaters tie in the long program, the nod goes to the one judged to be more artistic.

Prior to 1991, the short program consisted of "compulsory figures," which required skaters to perform a set of maneuvers that were graded for technical achievement only. It usually took a skater several years before she could master these skills. Also, it gave judges a chance to reward or punish competitors for things that had nothing to do with the program. After much criticism, the rule was changed to allow for a more interesting (and in many ways less demanding) short program. This opened the door to younger skaters, who could perform more athletic spins, jumps, and combinations. And it changed the sport forever.

Debi Thomas won the bronze medal at the 1988 Olympics, then quit skating to study medicine at Stanford University. Despite Debi's example, it has become increasingly difficult for skaters to live a "normal" life.

an edge with the judges. Fratianne got a nose job, while Potzsch had 10 pounds surgically removed. Potzsch won the gold medal in the closest competition up to that time.

The 1980s saw the first African-American world champion in Debi Thomas, who began attracting attention when she pulled off a perfect triple jump at the age of 11. Unlike most promising youngsters, Thomas refused to give herself up to the "skating machine" that exists in most countries. She wanted a normal life, with normal friends, and a normal school. She lived and competed on her own terms, and it paid off. She won the world title in 1986, handing Katarina Witt her only international defeat, and took the U.S. Championships twice. In preparation for the 1988 Olympics, Thomas asked ballet star Mikhail Baryshnikov for help, and he "lent" her one of his choreographers. She was favored to win the gold, but messed up a couple of jumps in her long program and had to settle for a bronze medal. Thomas ended up a big winner, however, when she left the sport with her sanity.

That is not an easy thing to do. For every world-famous skater, there are hundreds of young women—who train just as hard and risk just as much—that do not make it. This is true in almost every sport, of course, but in skating the failures often have lifelong consequences. The annual cost of financing a promising skater's career can be more than many people make in a year. Countless families have taken on extra jobs and extra debt, and put their lives in limbo for their daughters—gambling everything on one of the most daunting "longshots" in all of sports. Needless to say, this puts unimaginable pressure on girls who should not have to think of such things. It is hard enough to concentrate on skating—think of how hard it would be to land a triple jump knowing that, if you fall, your family might lose its house. It has happened more than once.

There are, of course, a lot of happy stories in the world of women's figure skating. Some do not start out that way, but then the road to a championship is not supposed to be an easy one. The skaters profiled in the following pages have redefined their sport over the past 15 years, and continue to do so, both as amateurs and professionals.

ON HER MIND

"Work, work, work... and you will accomplish everything you want."

Oksana Baiul

The world of sports is full of "Cinderella Stories"—those magical, rags-to-riches tales of the athlete nobody wanted or the team nobody knew beating the odds to become a champion. But is anyone's story more like Cinderella than Oksana Baiul's? She grew up in Ukraine, which was part of the Soviet Union. Her father disappeared mysteriously when she was two, and she was raised by her mother and grandparents. Oksana began skating at the age of three, and by her eighth birthday was one of the top young skaters in the country. She could land jumps and perform spins that other girls her age were afraid to attempt.

What should have been a happy story, however, started to go terribly wrong. Her grandfather died when she was nine, and her grandmother passed away a year later. When Oksana was 13, her mother died, too. She was alone and scared. Stanislav Korytek, her skating coach, continued to teach her, and a family friend looked after her as best she could. But basically, Oksana was on her own.

Things got worse before they got better. The Soviet Union was disintegrating, and its once-vaunted sports programs were in total disarray. In an earlier time, Oksana would have been shipped off to a state training center. But now there was no money left for young skaters, and the political situation in Ukraine was very unstable. In 1992, when Oksana was 14, Korytek decided to leave the country and take a coaching job in Canada. Fearing

Oksana has really grown as an artist since her Olympic triumph in 1994.

Oksana practices at the 1994 Olympics. A short time later, she collided with a German skater, putting her medal chances in doubt.

Oksana would "slip through the cracks," he asked fellow instructor Galina Zmievskaya to take his young pupil into her home. She agreed. It was Oksana's first lucky break in a long, long time.

Oksana left her home for the city of Odessa, 250 miles away. There she met Zmievskaya's prize pupil, Viktor Petrenko. Many considered him the best skater in the world, and he immediately became a "big brother" to Oksana. He bought her new skates, a blade sharpener, and gave her leftover material from his costumes so she could make new ones for herself. Oksana started to feel good about her world again, and it showed in her skating. She improved dramatically in her new environment, and in 1993 she entered her first senior skating competition, the Ukrainian nationals. The little dynamo gave a heart-stopping performance and won the event. In her first international competition, Oksana finished second to Surya Bonaly at the 1993 European Championships.

That win made Oksana eligible to compete in the World Championships, in the Czech Republic. She went to Prague a complete unknown and "ambushed" the top skaters by winning the gold medal. The crowds watched, totally stunned, as Oksana burst upon the international scene before their eyes. The other skaters were awestruck, too.

It did not seem possible that a "nobody from nowhere" could possess so much talent. Indeed, despite her age, Oksana seemed to have everything—jumping skills, technical precision, artistic maturity, a great personality, and a smile that made judges putty in her hands. And, of course, a story that the press adored.

Next, Oksana embarked on a long exhibition tour of the U.S. with Petrenko and other top skaters. She won Skate America, the biggest international event held in North America, and gained confidence and experience as she headed for the Olympics. She even got to tour with Jill Trenary, her idol. It had been a little more than a year since Oksana's plight seemed hopeless. Now, she was on top of the world.

There were, however, some drawbacks to her newfound fame. As the 1994 Olympics approached, Oksana began to feel the pressure of being in

Getting Personal

Oksana was born on November 16, 1977, in Dnepropetrovsk, Ukraine...At the age of three, she laced up her first pair of skates after her mother tried to enroll her in a ballet class. The instructor said she was too chubby, and should try figure skating...Oksana gave up ballet after her first skating meet. "When I was seven," she says, "I won my first competition, so I decided to stay in figure skating."...Her mother, Marina, was diagnosed with ovarian cancer in 1991 and died within a year...Oksana had always believed her father was dead, and was shocked when he reappeared at her mom's funeral. He then disappeared from her life again...Her world championship at the age of 15 made her the youngest winner in nearly 70 years...When Oksana moved in with Coach Zmievskaya, it made a cramped situation downright crowded! Zmievskaya and her husband lived in a three-room apartment with their two daughters, a dog, and a parrot...The first time Viktor Petrenko saw Oksana, he knew she could be a champion. He was horrified to hear that she had not had new skate blades in four years...She turned professional after the 1994 Olympics. Since then, her repertoire has grown to include everything from classical programs to funky jazz routines...In 1997, Oksana got behind the wheel of a car after drinking too much, and crashed at 100 mph. She was lucky to survive. Some said she was so burnt out on being a superstar that she crashed on purpose. Oksana dismisses these notions as ridiculous, and says, "I don't want the car accident to be the end of my life. It's not a tragedy. It's just a test."

Career Highlights	
Year	Achievement
1993	Silver Medalist, European Championships
1993	World Champion
1994	Silver Medalist, European Championships
1994	Olympic Gold Medalist

the spotlight. Every place she went, people told her she could win the gold medal. Whenever she did an interview, one of the first questions was almost always, "What do you have to do to win the gold?" Oksana began to wonder herself. And she started to worry.

Just before the games began, Oksana stopped being the biggest story in skating. Nancy Kerrigan was attacked prior to the U.S. Championships, and it looked as if another skater, Tonya Harding, might have been involved in the plot. Oksana was sad for Nancy; she had been through some tough times herself, but no one had ever assaulted her. Still, it turned out to be a lucky break. Oksana was able to prepare for the Olympics without hordes of reporters following her every move. And her two main rivals for the gold—Kerrigan and Harding—had had their lives turned upside down.

When the Olympics began, Kerrigan made a miraculous comeback and performed as well as she ever had. She finished ahead of Oksana in the short program, setting up an epic showdown on the last night. The long program was not Kerrigan's strong point, but she was skating so well everyone was sure she would give a memorable performance. Meanwhile, Oksana—who considered the free skate her specialty—was nursing a painful injury. The day before the finals, she had collided with Germany's Tanja Szewczenko and suffered cuts on her right leg and a sore back.

Kerrigan skated her final routine even better than expected, putting the pressure on Oksana. She took two pain-killing injections before she hit the ice, and then began. Skating to a medley of Broadway tunes, Oksana ripped off jump after jump, gaining confidence with each small triumph. By the end of her routine she was so psyched that she actually added an extra triple jump. Oksana had not only skated a near-flawless program, she had skated from the heart. Four judges gave Kerrigan the points she needed to win, but five sided with Oksana. It was the closest finish in Olympic history, but Oksana won the gold. Cinderella had her glass slipper.

Oksana is flanked by fellow Olympic medalists Nancy Kerrigan (left) and Chen Lu after her big night in Lillehammer.

ON HER MIND

"In other sports they don't care how you run. You're faster and that's it. It's not about your dress."

Surya Bonaly

C hange is usually a slow, steady process in sports. It is a natural result of one competitor trying to outdo all the others. This has certainly been true in figure skating. After Sonja Henie introduced jumping to the skating world, every subsequent advance has represented a small step forward. Then along came French sensation Surya Bonaly. At the age of 16 she was performing moves that no one else could do a decade later. Surya's story is, in many ways, just as fantastic and improbable as her amazing skating style.

Back in the 1970s, Surya's parents, Suzanne and Georges, were disturbed by the number of homeless kids they saw on their trips to India. So they decided to adopt a French child rather than have one of their own. Surya skated for the first time at the age of two. "I was the only baby who had feet big enough to fit into figure skates," she says of that first time on the ice. "It was a big joke at the rink."

Although Surya loved skating, it was not initially her best sport. She excelled in gymnastics, and was a first-rate tumbler and trampolinist. Surya never lost her love of the ice, however, and yearned to apply what she had learned as a gymnast to figure skating. In 1984, when she was 10 years old, French skating coach Didier Gailhaguet spotted her at a rink near her home, in Nice. He told the Bonalys that she could be a champion, and convinced them to move to Paris, where Surya could receive the best instruction. Thus began one of the most bizarre and controversial careers in all of sports.

Surya and her parents were considered very weird. They loved animals, and traveled from event to event in a van with their five dogs.

Surya takes a break during a workout. She does things no one else in the sport even dares to try.

Surya dazzles the crowd at the 1996 European Championships. She has won this competition four times.

Sometimes there were doves, too. There is even a story about Suzanne giving CPR to a bear after it was hit by a car! The family rarely stayed in hotels and ate a macrobiotic diet that included birdseed. Surya's mother knew nothing about figure skating, yet made all the decisions, from routines to costumes to make-up to music. All of these details are crucial in figure skating, because the difference between victory and defeat is measured in tenths and hundredths of points. Some said Suzanne had no business making such important decisions.

The Bonalys would have been the laughingstock of the skating world were it not for one thing: Surya blew her rivals out of the rink. She was strong, and fast and powerful, and she could land jumps and string together combinations that made audiences gasp. Surya was different from her rivals in another way: She had dark skin. Some believe prejudice may have been a factor when the judges gave her low scores for her athletic routines. They said she was "too athletic" and not artistic enough.

Proud, stubborn, and convinced she was in the right, Surya refused to change and kept right on winning. In 1990, at the age of 16, she was crowned French champion. In 1991, she won the World Junior Championships, as well as her first of four straight European titles. By the time the 1992 Winter Olympics began in Albertville, France, Surya was the hottest athlete in the country. The international media became obsessed with her.

This attention backfired, however, when Surya failed to win a medal for France. Though physically superior to the other skaters, she lacked the artistic expression Olympic judges demand. She finished a disappointing fifth, and the French press pounded her. A series of coaches followed, but none was willing to put up with the constant meddling by Suzanne, who was unwilling to relinquish control of her daughter's career.

Despite this instability, Surya continued to improve in all areas. Her performances showed more depth and emotion. In 1994, she returned to the Olympic stage and did well, but was bumped out of the medals race when Oksana Baiul, Nancy Kerrigan, and Chen Lu turned in the performances of their lives. Frustrated, Surya lost her cool a few weeks later at the World Championships in Japan. She had completed what everyone agreed was her all-time best routine, but finished second to Japanese star Yuka Sato. Feeling she had been the victim of "hometown" favoritism, Surya ripped her silver medal off during the awards ceremony.

Getting Personal

Surya was born on December 15, 1973, in Nice, France...She was adopted by the Bonalys eight months later...Her parents were interested in eastern religions such as Zen and Taoism. To this day Surya signs her name with a yin-yang symbol beside it...Surya was the 1985 world junior tumbling champion...In her early years as a skater, she would sometimes spend 12 hours a day at the practice rink...She landed her first quadruple jump in practice when she was 16...In order to stir up interest in Surya prior to the 1992 Olympics, her coach fabricated stories about her being found "amongst the coconuts" on the French-held island of Reunion, near Madagascar. The Bonalys actually adopted her from an orphanage in Nice...At the 1992 Winter Games she was accorded the honor of giving the athlete's oath to all of the Olympic competitors...Surya is 5' 3" and weighs 105 pounds. She has the most rock-solid body in her sport...Of the endless criticism she and her mother endure, Surya says, "Maybe it's better to have things this way. It makes us strong"...Surya has been skating with the Champions on Ice tour.

Career Highlights

Year	Achievement
1991	World Junior Champion
1991	European Champion
1992	European Champion
1993	European Champion
1993	Silver Medalist, World Championships
1994	European Champion
1994	Trophee de France Champion
1994	Silver Medalist, World Championships
1995	European Champion
1995	Silver Medalist, World Championships

It is hard to imagine what Surya was going through. She was—and still is—the only female skater in the world who can perform a backflip and a quadruple jump. She knew these moves were outlawed because they are considered too dangerous, but continued to perform them to the great delight of her fans. This did not ingratiate her to the international skating community, which had to answer the same uncomfortable question every time Surya performed one of her dazzling routines. Everyone knew that, some day, backflips and quadruple jumps would be part of women's figure skating, so why not now?

In May of 1996, Surya snapped her Achilles tendon while practicing a backflip. She could probably hear the "I told you so's" before she even hit the ground. It would have been perfectly understandable had she called it a career right then and there—why kill yourself coming back from a devastating injury, only to put up with the same old garbage? But quitting was not in Surya. She came back to win her ninth national title in 1997, and qualified for the Olympic Games in 1998. "I can say to myself and other sportsmen who are injured, it's okay—you can do it after a big injury," Surya says with pride. "You can come back to the highest level."

At Nagano in 1998, Surya was out of the running for a medal after a so-so short program. When it came time to skate her long routine, she decided to make a little history. She started like she had been shot out of a cannon, and proceeded to give the crowd a glimpse of the future. Surya showed off everything in her repertoire, including a backflip she landed on one skate. As usual, she was awe-inspiring. She dropped from sixth to 10th, but says it was worth it.

What Surya accomplishes from here—and how she fits into sports history—should make an interesting conclusion to a fascinating story. Those who witnessed her virtuosity will one day tell their grandchildren about the woman who could fly, about the skater who could make her body do anything. Thank goodness for videotape. Those grandkids probably won't believe them!

If ever a picture were worth a thousand words, this would be the one. Surya goes airborne during the 1998 Olympics in Nagano, Japan. Years from now, it may rank among the true ground-breaking moments in women's sports.

Nancy Kerrigan

A lot of kids dream about being a superstar athlete. Yet few understand how complicated life can be when you are nearing the top of your sport. The press wants you, the fans want you, the sport itself wants you—and all the while, your competitors are doing everything they can to knock you on your behind. By the time Nancy Kerrigan started gaining recognition as a world-class athlete, she had no illusions about the cut-throat world of figure skating. But that did not prepare her for one of the most shocking episodes in the history of competitive sports.

Nancy grew up in Stoneham, Massachusetts. The Kerrigan kids always seemed to be on the ice. Her two older brothers were good hockey players, and Nancy began showing she would be a special skater around the age of six. Her father worked extra jobs and took out loans so Nancy could pursue her dream of winning an Olympic medal. Nancy worked hard, too, sometimes getting to the skating rink before sunrise so she could get in a couple of hours of practice before school started.

Although Nancy could execute difficult maneuvers at a young age, she was not considered a "prodigy." It took eight years before she could do well in major competitions, but each year she learned something new and added more complexity to her programs. In the fall of 1988, she took first place at events in Austria and Hungary, then placed fifth at the 1989 U.S. Championships. By this time she had graduated from high school and was practicing 60 to 70 hours a week.

Few athletes in history have met challenges with as much determination and heart as Nancy Kerrigan.

More than 300 journalists—10 times the normal number—jammed Nancy's first practice after her attack. Her remarkable comeback was good for a silver medal a few days later.

At the 1990 nationals, Nancy finished third in the short and long programs, but failed to win a medal because she got a case of the jitters in the compulsory figures, which counted for 20 percent of her score. Most skaters would have been crestfallen, but Nancy says it was a turning point for her. "I realized that I was now as good as the three skaters who had finished ahead of me," she remembers. "But I was still bothered by nervousness when the time came to show the judges what I could do."

Nancy sensed what was holding her back. She was afraid of putting it all on the line. She did not want to give everything and have the judges tell her it was not enough. Once she got over that hurdle, she became a star. In 1991, Nancy placed third in the nationals behind Kristi Yamaguchi and Tonya Harding. At the World Championships, Nancy finished a surprising third behind Yamaguchi and Harding again, and suddenly people began taking the "new Nancy" very, very seriously. In the fall of 1991, Nancy took on the top skaters in the world and this time she won, placing first at the prestigious Nations Cup. At the 1992 U.S. Championships, she finished second to Yamaguchi to qualify for the Olympics.

This was Nancy's dream, and she made the most of the opportunity. She hung around with other athletes, attended different events, and had the time of her life at the Olympic Village in Albertville, France. Then, when the skating started, Nancy put on a glorious show. After the short program she was in second place, behind Yamaguchi. In the long program, however, Nancy lost her balance for just an instant, costing her precious points. She had to settle for the bronze medal. Nancy was pleased, but vowed to go for the gold at the 1994 Winter Games.

In the interim, Nancy won the 1993 U.S. Championships and was skating well heading into the 1994 nationals. This became a matter of great concern in the Tonya Harding camp, particularly for Harding's on-again, off-again husband, Jeff Gillooly. Gillooly felt that the only person standing between Tonya and a gold medal (and thus his own fame and fortune), was Nancy. Gillooly and bodyguard Shawn Eckhardt arranged to have a thug named Shane Stant injure Nancy seriously enough to keep her out of the Olympics.

At a practice session in Detroit, Stant ambushed Nancy as she came off the ice and smashed her right knee with a heavy metal rod. "I tried to

Getting Personal

Nancy was born on October 13, 1969...Nancy's mom contracted a rare virus when Nancy was two. It caused her to lose a good deal of her sight and is legally blind. She can only see Nancy skate if she puts her face very close to the television screen...As a kid, Nancy's favorite stuffed animal was a monkey named Melvin. She still has Melvin today...Her patented move is the extended spiral, a difficult combination of balance and power...Family has always been the most important thing to Nancy. While growing up, nearly 100 relatives lived within a two-hour drive...Nancy is reminded of her incredible ordeal whenever a bizarre news story hits the airwaves. She says, "I think, 'I was part of something like that?' It doesn't even seem real to me"...Nancy raised a lot of eyebrows when she agreed to appear with Tonya Harding in a 1998 television special called "Breaking the Ice: The Women of '94 Revisited." Tonya saw it as a way to make a quick buck, while Nancy saw it as—what else?— yet another challenge.

Career *Highlights*

Year	Achievement
1991	Bronze Medalist, U.S. Championships
1991	Nations Cup Champion
1992	Silver Medalist, U.S. Championships
1992	Silver Medalist, World Championships
1992	Olympic Bronze Medalist
1993	U.S. Champion
1994	Olympic SIlver Medalist

take a couple of steps but the pain was indescribable," Nancy remembers. "Suddenly, the world of skating as I knew it had changed."

Luckily, Nancy was not injured badly. While she recuperated in the hospital, the whole weird story unfolded. The dastardly trio had left clues all over the place, and the police quickly closed in on them. Nancy was shocked to find that Harding might have been involved; to this day her role in the assault, if any, has never been proved.

Needless to say, the "Kerrigan Assault" became the world's top news story. The media just would not let it go. The two skaters were cast as bitter rivals. Tonya was eviscerated by the press and characterized as a dumb, low-class Kerrigan "wannabe." Nancy was presented as being aloof, and called the "Ice Princess." Although the incident focused unprecedented attention on the sport of figure skating, it turned the Olympic competition into a three-ring circus. Nancy recovered in time to fly to Lillehammer, Norway, and was given a spot on the U.S. team. This time she could not go anywhere in the Olympic Village without being mobbed by reporters and curiosity seekers.

Finally, it was time to hit the ice. With a record number of people watching, Nancy skated as well as she ever had in her life, with her lone flaw being a double jump where she had originally planned a triple. Only a miraculous performance by 16-year-old Oksana Baiul kept Nancy from winning the gold medal.

Would Nancy have done better had she been 100 percent? Could she have won the gold? "Would have" and "could have" are not part of competitive skating. Nancy says she was disappointed but, "I realized that making it to the Olympics so soon after what happened was a victory in itself. I had done two of the best programs of my life."

A big reason Nancy was able to pull herself together during this terrible ordeal was the steady hand of her agent and friend, Jerry Solomon. A year later, they were married, and in December of 1996 they had a son named Matthew. Nancy, who had joined the professional skating tour after the Olympics, took time off to get back in shape for the 1998 season. "Having a baby is like using a Mercedes instead of a pickup truck to carry lumber and cement around a construction project," she laughs. "The Mercedes does the job, but afterward it doesn't run quite the same."

Nancy did indeed return to the ice in '98, splitting time between touring and spending time with her family. She wants to keep skating, for herself and for the millions who cheered her throughout her career. She also wants to have two more kids.

And why not? After all, no one takes on a challenge like Nancy Kerrigan!

Nancy and Jerry Solomon tie the knot in September of 1995. They now have a son named Matthew.

On Her Mind

"Instead of worrying about what will happen, I just go out and skate. That's what I always want to do—just go out and skate."

Michelle Kwan

Some athletes take a long time to develop a competitive edge. Others seem to have it from the start. As soon as Michelle Kwan started taking figure skating lessons, she began winning competitions. Her first came at the age of six. At the age of seven, she watched Brian Boitano win the gold medal at the 1988 Olympics and began setting her sights a little higher. Her sister, Karen, also shared this dream.

The Kwans knew they had two talented and highly focused little girls on their hands. In 1990, the year Michelle turned 10, they decided to hire top coach Frank Carroll. After a year, Carroll told the Kwans that Michelle had the potential to be an Olympian. Michelle went to live and train with other promising skaters in Lake Arrowhead, California. There she practiced three hours a day, seven days a week. Michelle also had a tutor so she could keep up in her studies.

By 1992, Michelle was considered one of the rising stars in junior skating. She believed she could compete at an even higher level. One day, while Coach Carroll was out of town, she took the test for admission to senior-level events, performing a series of moves for a panel of judges. Although Michelle passed, her coach was furious. How, he wanted to know, could a girl who finished ninth in the juniors expect to compete against more experienced skaters? Michelle answered that question the only way she knew how: by winning. She was victorious at four major events, including the 1993 Olympic Festival, where she charmed a crowd of 25,000—the largest in the history of figure skating.

Michelle always wears a special dragon pendant for good luck. It was given to her by her grandmother.

Michelle's performance at the 1998 Olympics was good for a silver medal. Most experts agree that, in any other year, it would have been good enough to win the gold.

At the 1994 U.S. Championships, Michelle finished second. Normally, this would have guaranteed her a spot on the Olympic team, as the U.S. was sending two skaters to Lillehammer that year. But Michelle's spot was given to Nancy Kerrigan, who had missed the competition after being attacked in a plot to knock her out of the Olympics. Michelle ended up going to Norway as an alternate. She prepared and practiced as if she would be competing, but as it turned out she did not get to skate.

With no choice but to aim for the 1998 Olympics, Michelle set out to become the world's best skater during the four-year interim. During that time, however, she had to deal with a lot more than toe loops and triple jumps. Figure skating can be a tricky business, especially for teenagers. A young woman's body can change from month to month, and in a sport that demands such incredible precision, those slight differences really test a skater's ability to adjust. In Michelle's case, the adjustments did not come easily. From 1993 to 1995, she grew seven inches and gained about 20 pounds. Finally, in 1995, she reached her full height of 5' 2", and her weight leveled off at around 100 pounds. In 1995 and 1996, Michelle came into her own. She won the Skate

Canada, Skate America, and Nations Cup competitions in '95, and in '96 she put the finishing touches on her smooth, flowing style by achieving an ideal balance between emotion and poise.

In 1996, Michelle entered the World Championships. Her goal was to unseat defending champion Chen Lu. After skating a brilliant opening routine, Michelle was in excellent position to win. But Chen skated a long program that earned several perfect 6s. With the pressure on, Michelle took the ice with the soul of a bird and the heart of a warrior. She landed six triple jumps, and then sealed the deal with an unplanned—and unrehearsed—triple toe loop at the end of her program to win the gold. "Nothing could stop me," she remembers. "If a brick wall had been on the ice, I would have just rammed through it."

For the new world champ, 1997 should have been a great year. But it was not. She fell twice at the U.S. Championships and lost event after event to up-and-coming Tara Lipinski. Nagging injuries further sapped Michelle's confidence. Yet during this frustrating year, she actually gained a little perspective. At the 1997 World Championships, she messed up

Getting Personal

Michelle was born on July 7, 1980, in Torrance, California...She has a brother, Ron, and a sister, Karen...The Kwan girls first hit the ice after watching their older brother at a hockey practice. Michelle was only five...Her parents sold their home so they could afford the $60,000 annual cost of Michelle's career...When Michelle started winning big events, her fans would throw stuffed animals on the ice after her programs...One of the biggest adjustments Michelle had to make as a world-class skater was wearing makeup. "I was afraid to jump with mascara on," she giggles, "I didn't think I'd be able to see!"...Michelle enjoyed another victory in the spring of 1998: she received her high school diploma. Her GPA for the first semester of her senior year was a perfect 4.0...After the Olympics she signed a four-year deal with Disney. "To be a part of the Disney family is a dream come true," she says...Can Michelle compete with the teen sensations in 2002? She believes she can. "I want to show that being 21 isn't too old," Michelle says.

Career *Highlights*

Year	Achievement
1993	Gold Medalist, 1993 Olympic Festival
1994	Silver Medalist, U.S. Championships
1995	Nations Cup Champion
1996	World Champion
1997	Silver Medalist, World Championships
1998	U.S. Champion
1998	Olympic Silver Medalist
1998	World Champion

her short program so badly that she had no chance of defending her title. Afterwards, in the locker room, Michelle broke a lace while tying her sneakers, and accidentally punched herself in the face. For most people, this would have been the last straw. For Michelle, it seemed to knock a little sense into her. She started laughing. So I botched a jump, she thought, is that the end of my life? Of course not. Reinvigorated, Michelle skated a dazzling long program and made it all the way back to second place. "I was the happiest silver medalist ever," she remembers.

At the 1998 U.S. Championships, Michelle shook off a stress fracture to one of her toes and turned in the best performance of her life. She landed no fewer than seven perfect triple jumps, and skated with unparalleled artistry. Eight of the nine judges gave her 6s for her presentation; in all, she received 15 perfect marks during the event. "I never saw so many 6s in my life," she remembers. "I was nailing everything. I landed every jump with a smile—when I got on the ice I knew I was having fun and enjoying my performance."

Going into the Olympics, Michelle was a slight favorite over Lipinski, who had also skated a lights-out long program at the nationals. When the competition began, Michelle was technically brilliant, but the pressure of being the gold-medal favorite and concern over her foot seemed to take the joy out of her skating. She won the short program, but in the long program she had a slight wobble after one of her triple jumps. Otherwise,

Michelle had skated flawlessly—certainly well enough to win at any other Olympics. But an other-worldly performance by Lipinski enabled her to edge Michelle out of the top spot by the slimmest of margins. Michelle could not help wondering what the outcome might have been had she skated pain-free.

At the 1998 World Championships, she found out. Feeling as good as she had in a couple of years, Michelle skated with her old joy and won her second world title. She was not perfect, but perfection has become less important to Michelle, who now feels that the real goal in each competition is laying it on the line, enjoying herself and doing her very best.

As for the future, figure skating fans should be seeing a lot of Michelle. While Tara turned pro a few months after the Olympics, Michelle decided to stay in the game and find out just how good she can be. "There are other competitors," she says of life without Lipinski. "Maybe there's another 13-year-old coming up. You never know!"

Besides, as Michelle sees it, there is still another Olympic medal to be won. "There's another 'golden opportunity' coming up in 2002," she smiles. "If I don't go, I'll probably regret it."

Michelle and her coach celebrate her victory at the 1996 World Championships.

ON HER MIND

"I wouldn't want to have the same life that everyone else has. I love my life. Skating is what I do."

Tara Lipinski

Ten years ago, a figure skater celebrating her 21st birthday had every reason to believe she was in her prime. Thanks to Tara Lipinski, today's 21-year-olds must feel like prime candidates for the old age home. At 14, Tara became the youngest world champion in the history of her sport, and at 15 she became the youngest athlete to win a Winter Olympic gold medal in any sport.

Unlike today's other top skaters, Tara began her career on wheels. An accomplished roller-blader at the age of three, she graduated to the ice when she was six. After only an hour, Tara was executing the same turns and jumps she had perfected on the pavement. The Lipinskis, who lived in southern New Jersey, took Tara for lessons at the University of Delaware's skating center, which ranks among the best in the country.

When Tara was nine, her father was transferred to Houston, Texas. The family purchased a house in nearby Sugarland and Tara continued her skating at the Galleria, a fancy shopping mall in Houston. The mall was too noisy during the day, so Tara would wake up at three in the morning and squeeze in a few hours of practice before school. Sometimes, though, she had no choice but to practice while shoppers were there. It takes incredible focus to perform figure skating maneuvers, and a busy mall is probably the worst place to practice. Yet it may have been these very conditions that enabled Tara to develop the concentration of a champion before she reached her teens.

The Lipinskis were astounded at Tara's progress. So was her coach, Megan Faulkner. She told Tara's parents that she deserved better than

Tara and her dog, Coco, enjoy a golden moment during a "Welcome Home" celebration after the Olympics.

Tara skates with such remarkable poise and maturity it is easy to forget she is just a kid.

what was available in Houston. Jack Lipinski, however, could not leave his job.

The family made a hard decision: Tara and her mother would move back east and rent a small apartment near the Delaware rink. Her father would stay in Texas and send money to support her training. Although they talked every night on the phone and saw each other once a month, Tara and her dad missed each other desperately.

The good news was that the move paid off a lot sooner than anyone imagined. Working with coach Jeff DiGregorio, Tara learned how to launch herself into the air and do quick, tight spins that bigger skaters could not. She could twirl around, hit the ice, then pop right back into the air for another difficult jump, landing combinations that were unheard of for a skater her age.

Tara placed second in the national novice competition at age 11, and at age 12 won the gold medal in the junior division of the 1994 Olympic Festival. Suddenly, everyone in America wanted to know everything about this little sprite. Newspapers ran feature stories on Tara, and she appeared on network television shows. At the junior nationals that year, Tara opened a lot of eyes when she executed a perfect triple jump.

For Tara to take the next step, the Lipinskis decided she needed a new coach. They selected Richard Callaghan. Tara and her mom moved to Detroit, Michigan, where he was based, and began preparing for the 1996 U.S. Championships. One of Callaghan's other skaters, Todd Eldridge, had won the 1995 nationals. He and Tara would have contests to see who was the best jumper. Incredibly, she was able to do everything Eldridge could do. Tara only weighed 70 pounds, but her body was flexible and her muscles were strong. She did not get as high off the ice as other skaters, but she spun faster. By the time Tara reached the '96 nationals, this signature style had earned her the nickname "Leapin' Lipinski." Tara finished third at the U.S. Championships, behind Michelle Kwan and Tonia Kwiatkowski, and received big ovations after each of her programs.

During the summer of 1996, Tara worked on looking a little older. She did not want judges dismissing her as a kid, so she undertook a major

Getting Personal

Tara was born on June 10, 1982, in Philadelphia, Pennsylvania...she has no brothers or sisters...Before she began ice skating, Tara was a terror in street hockey games...Tara's tastes are a little more grown-up now that she is a teenager. Her favorite food used to be grapes with whipped cream, M&Ms, and sprinkles on top...Tara never knew what to expect when she skated at Houston's Galleria. Once she arrived to find a gigantic Christmas tree in the middle of the rink!...In order for Tara to be crowned 1997 World Champion, an old rule had to be waived. You had to be 15 years old to compete...Her favorite athletes are Michael Jordan, Tiger Woods, and gymnast Dominique Moceanu...At the 1998 Olympics, Tara and Michelle Kwan gave the U.S. its first gold-silver women's skating combo in 42 years...Tara's mom described her daughter's reaction to winning the gold her "Publisher's Clearing House scream"...Though she stands just 4' 10", Tara is quite an athlete. "I just love sports," she says. "Ballet, jazz dance, gymnastics, tennis, horseback riding...I'm not good at everything. Some things I'm a total mess at"...Tara plans to go to college one day. She has not decided what she will study...Tara has a major collection of Beanie Babies.

Career *Highlights*

Year	Achievement
1997	U.S. Champion
1997	World Champion
1998	Silver Medalist, U.S. Championships
1998	Olympic Gold Medalist

transformation. Off came the ponytail and on went the makeup—not too much, just enough to look sophisticated. Her wardrobe and music changed, too. Where Tara made the most progress, however, was on the ice. She was skating with more maturity and feeling. She wanted to be known for ballet-like grace as well as her spectacular jumping ability.

The new Tara debuted at Skate Canada in the fall of 1996. The judges were impressed, and awarded her the silver medal—her first in international competition. The following week she won a bronze medal in Paris, and a week after that another silver medal at the prestigious Nations Cup in Germany. At the 1997 U.S. Championships, Tara landed an incredibly difficult triple lutz/double loop combination during her short program, then pulled off a mind-boggling triple loop/triple loop during her long program to win the championship. From there, Tara went to Switzerland for the World Championships. Once again, she skated two magnificent programs and won the gold medal. No one—not even the great Sonja Henie—had ever won the worlds at such a young age.

As the 1998 season got under way, some fans were discounting Tara's accomplishments. Michelle Kwan had had an off year in 1997, but seemed to be back on track by the time the '98 nationals began. Their showdown was front-page news. Never before had two skaters so young battled for the U.S. championship. This time, Kwan prevailed. Tara fell during her short program, while Michelle skated mistake-free. The bad news for Tara was a second-place finish. The good news was that she had made the Olympic team.

The 1998 Winter Olympics in Nagano, Japan, quickly turned into the "Tara and Michelle Show." It was all anyone could talk about. Tara had played the role of precocious pixie, and she also had skated as an odds-on favorite. But she had never really been an "underdog." In this case, at least, the role seemed to suit her. Tara was relaxed and open. While Kwan stayed with her family in a hotel outside the Olympic Village, Tara had a blast. She hung around with the other athletes, went shopping, and even answered her e-mail at the communications center. By the time she took the ice, she was beaming with enthusiasm.

Kwan skated tremendously, but seemed a little nervous. Tara was brilliant, too. "When I stepped on the ice I had a feeling I knew what the Olympics were about," she says. "I had that feeling of pure joy, and I went out there and put it in my program." After Tara finished her final skate, no one knew who had won—it was that close. When her scores came up, Tara shrieked with surprise and delight. She was the youngest Olympic champion ever. In the end, it was her triple loop/triple loop and surprising maturity that swayed the judges. Many believe that her long program was the best ever at the Olympics.

Today, Tara is the world's most popular professional skater. The decision to turn pro was easy for her—it meant she could repay all of the money her parents had spent...and best of all, the Lipinskis could be a family again!

Tara is already skating like a seasoned pro. It is hard to believe she has accomplished so much in such a short time.

"I love almost all the things about my country. It is just a few problems with a few people. That is not enough to make me hate my whole country."

Chen Lu

very so often, we begin to take our freedom for granted. Then along comes someone like Chen Lu to remind us just how precious it is. What she endured in order to compete in two Olympics earned her a permanent place in the hearts of skating fans everywhere. What she did once she got there nailed down a page in the record books.

Lu grew up in Changchun, an industrial city in northeast China located above North Korea. Her parents were both accomplished athletes—her mom had been a successful table tennis player and her father was a member of China's national hockey team. Lu often accompanied her father to practice, and this is where she first became acquainted with skating. By the age of five, she was totally at home on the ice and began showing the kind of promise that made her parents believe she had a future in the sport.

Unfortunately, China had no training or coaching program, and there was not a single indoor rink in the entire country. Lu had to wait for the temperature to drop each winter so she could work out on a flooded field near her home. She would skate until it got dark, with her father coaching her as best he could. "I could have gone longer, but there wasn't any light," she remembers fondly.

When Lu was eight, her parents found a proper rink for her to use. It was an outdoor facility and her ice time usually ran from midnight until 5 a.m. The temperature sometimes dipped to minus 20, but Lu was so

No one was ever happier to win a bronze medal than Lu. She finished third at the 1998 Olympics after nearly failing to qualify.

Few skaters can claim to be "poetry in motion." Lu is most definitely one of them.

caught up in skating that she hardly noticed the frigid conditions. There were other aspiring figure skaters in China at the time, but none like Lu. When she skated, she seemed totally at peace, and completely natural. She was taking ballet classes, and tried her best to work what she learned into her skating. "I liked dance very much when I was little," she recalls. "Every time it was on TV, I would watch it."

Word of this wonderful young skater from the far-off province of Jilin reached the Chinese government, and at the age of nine Lu was moved closer to one of the country's new winter sports training centers. Figure skating was gaining popularity in China, and now there would be government-sponsored coaching and training for the most promising athletes. Lu began working with Li Mingzhu, a coach whose influence—both good and bad—she has felt ever since.

Although Lu started behind most of the other young skaters, she quickly surpassed them. She worked harder and just seemed to understand more about skating. After a year of top-level training Lu was landing difficult maneuvers, including triple jumps. China, which had never produced a single world-class skater, suddenly had a potential world champion on its hands. After Lu's 14th birthday, a decision was made to allow her to leave the country and train with Italy's Carlo Fassi, a legend in the sport. Fassi put the finishing touches on Lu and then set her loose on the world.

At the 1992 Olympics, Lu finished a surprising sixth. She also posted a pair of third-place finishes at the 1992 and '93 World Championships. By the time the 1994 Olympics came around, Lu was one of the sport's most admired and feared competitors.

At Lillehammer, she skated wonderfully in the short program, finishing a respectable third. In the long program, she was even better. The skater who stood between Lu and China's first figure skating medal was the spectacular Surya Bonaly. As all of China watched, Bonaly made a costly error in her program, giving Lu the bronze medal and setting off a wild celebration back home.

Lu squared off with Bonaly a year later, at the 1995 World Championships. The French star was at her best, but Lu had a surprise up her sleeve. As an Olympic medalist, Lu suddenly had access to some of the brightest minds in the sport, and she took full advantage of this opportunity. Among those Lu approached for advice was Toller Cranston, who assisted her with choreography. The former skater suggested Lu incorporate more of her own culture and heritage into her routines. When Lu took

Getting Personal

Lu was born on November 24, 1976, in Changchun, China...Her last name is Chen and first name Lu, but in the Chinese culture what we consider the "last name" always comes first...She has two sisters, Xue and Jie, but rarely sees them because she trains in far-off Beijing...Lu's skating technique has been described as "lyrical." According to famed coach Christy Ness, "It's unbelievable how close she comes to impersonating a butterfly"...Judges love the way Lu uses the ice—approaching jumps in unusual ways and taking angles other skaters do not...Lu's finest moment came at the 1996 World Championships, even though she placed second overall. She earned two perfect marks for her artistry in what many believe is one of the great long programs in the history of the sport...Recently she began calling herself Lu Chen, so as not to confuse western reporters... Her nickname is—what else?—Lu Lu!

Career *Highlights*

Year	Achievement
1992	Bronze Medalist, World Championships
1993	Bronze Medalist, World Championships
1994	Olympic Bronze Medalist
1995	World Champion
1996	Silver Medalist, World Championships
1998	Olympic Bronze Medalist

the ice for her final program, she gave a unique performance which was good enough to win the gold.

Lu continued to open eyes in the skating world, winning a medal at the World Championships for a fourth year in a row. But somewhere during what should have been a fabulous 1996 season, things started to go terribly wrong. In Communist China, citizens are supposed to be working for the greater glory of the nation. Also, any money earned by the few people allowed to leave the country is supposed to be turned over to the state. In the eyes of many Chinese leaders, Lu was grabbing too much of the glory for herself, and keeping too much money for "training and travel" expenses. They believed that she was no longer a source of pride for the Chinese people, but an object of envy. Worst of all her coach, Li, agreed. Lu began to falter under the strain of constant bickering, and by the time the 1997 season began, she was a mess. She was overweight, and was hobbled by recurring foot and ankle injuries. Lu was called back to China for "training" and "rehabilitation." Under the thumb of the Chinese government, she made little progress in the months she spent away from the figure skating world.

At the 1997 World Championships, she finished 25th and failed to qualify for the 1998 Olympics. Fearing her career was over, she broke down in the parking lot afterwards. Indeed, Lu was written off by most people—the tragic victim of a political system that no longer wanted her to win.

Fortunately, there was one last hope. A special Olympic qualifier was to be held in Vienna, Austria. Working with a new coach, Liu Hongyun, Lu got back in shape and skated well enough to win, earning a slot at Nagano. When she arrived in Japan, she looked like her old self again. She was smiling, relaxed and feeling no pressure at all. When the names of potential medalists came up, however, hers was rarely among them. That was fine with Lu. Once again, she had a surprise up her sleeve.

As Michelle Kwan and Tara Lipinski waged a high-profile battle for the gold medal, Lu quietly skated her way into contention. After the short program, she was in perfect position. If Tara and Michelle messed up, she could move right in and grab the gold. As it turned out, both skated brilliantly, taking the top two spots. But Lu locked up her second Olympic medal with an excellent long program to edge out European champion Maria Butyrskaya, who performed wonderfully herself.

Tears streamed down Lu's face as she stepped off the ice, and again as she mounted the podium to accept the bronze. "I wasn't looking for a medal," she insists. "I just wanted to prove to others I could still skate. I tried to skate with all my heart."

Lu is overcome with emotion after completing her spectacular long program at the 1998 Olympics in Nagano, Japan.

Katarina Witt

Every time a figure skater finishes her program, she receives two scores. One is for artistic beauty and the other for technical excellence. Katarina Witt comes as close as anyone to achieving the perfect balance between the two. That balance is what has kept her skating into her mid-30s, and it is what keeps people coming by the tens of thousands to watch her. Not surprisingly, the first time Katarina took the ice, she sensed that skating was something she was destined to do.

Bernd Egert, head coach at the sports school in Katarina's town, agreed. As soon as he saw her, he enrolled her in the school's intensive training program. This was quite an honor, but also a huge commitment. Sports schools in Communist East Germany were run by the government and resembled military bases. Children saw little of their families, and attended the school from seven in the morning until eight in the evening. In Katarina's case, four hours or more of that time was typically spent on the ice. The idea behind these "sports factories" was to produce experienced, hardened athletes who could dominate in international sports. Most kids "burned out." Those who survived, however, could become wealthy and famous in a political system geared toward keeping people poor and anonymous.

Katarina not only survived, she flourished. By the age of nine, she was training with Jutta Muller, East Germany's top skating coach. After two years with Muller, Katarina could execute a triple jump. And at the age of

Katarina, as "Carmen," shows off her gold medal at the 1988 Olympics.

Katarina gives Scott Hamilton a hug after skating a tribute to him in 1997. The two have known each other since they both won gold at the 1984 Olympics.

14 she made a name for herself by finishing 10th at the 1980 World Cham-pionships. It was extremely unusual for a girl so young to do so well. During this era, skaters had to perform a compulsory program of specific moves that typically took years to master. Rarely did an athlete under the age of 20 score well enough in this stage to finish in the Top 10 at international events. By the age of 17, however, Katarina had won the European Cham-pionships and finished second in the World Championships. Muller saw in her prize pupil the ability to be more than just a skater. She had Katarina perform "roles," ranging from gypsy princesses to flamenco dancers to belly dancers. Young Kat could hardly know it, but she was on the verge of revolutionizing her sport.

In 1984, Katarina won gold medals at the World Championships and the Winter Olympics, catapulting her to international fame. She stunned the judges with her artistry and poise, and her radiant personality captured the hearts of people all over the world. After the Olympics, she received 35,000 love letters! In the years that followed, Katarina showed that she could be a tough competitor—a quality she claims to have learned during those grueling years at the sports school. After finishing second to Debi Thomas at the World Championships in 1986, Katarina trained like a prize fighter so she would be ready for the 1987 event. In her final program, Katarina nailed one triple jump after another, and tried a pair of double axels, landing each of these risky maneuvers in perfect timing with the music. Even Thomas had to smile. She hated to lose, but it was an honor to be beaten by a performance like that.

The two squared off again at the 1988 Olympics. In what was billed as the "Battle of the Carmens," each woman chose to skate to music from Georges Bizet's classic opera, "Carmen." Thomas turned in a performance worthy of a gold medal in any other year. But Katarina—who had taken two years of acting lessons in preparation for this moment—was even better. She "became" Carmen and won the gold medal.

After the Olympics, Katarina returned to her home and started planning the rest of her life. She was 22, and already had achieved all of her childhood dreams. She had the beauty and charisma to become an actress, but in the end she decided to return to skating. After winning her

Getting Personal

Katarina was born on December 3, 1965, in Karl-Marx-Stadt, East Germany...Since the fall of Communism and German reunification, the town has reverted to its former name, Chemnitz...Her mother was a physical therapist and her father ran an agricultural cooperative. They agreed to give her skating lessons after she kept wandering away from her kindergarten class to watch skaters at a nearby arena...Katarina's brother, Axel, married Anett Potzsch. She too was a pupil of Jutta Muller's, and won a gold medal at the 1980 Olympics...Katarina's back-to-back Olympic gold medals marked the first time in more than 50 years that a skater accomplished this feat...In 1990, Katarina recreated her famous program for HBO's "Carmen on Ice" and won an Emmy Award for her performance...She has done color commentary for CBS, NBC, and several European networks...Katarina is still a huge drawing card for the Stars on Ice tour...She now has her own production company. Among her recent artistic projects was a film entitled "The Ice Princess." According to Katarina, "This is what I really love to do—putting together something from scratch."

Career Highlights

Year	Achievement
1983	European Champion
1984	European Champion
1984	World Champion
1984	Olympic Gold Medalist
1985	European Champion
1985	World Champion
1986	European Champion
1987	European Champion
1987	World Champion
1988	European Champion
1988	World Champion
1988	Olympic Gold Medalist

fourth and final World Championship, she joined the professional skating tour and headlined a show that included American gold medalist Brian Boitano. Free to concentrate on her creative interpretations of musical works and dramatic characters, Katarina's skating was more breathtaking than ever.

In the late 1980s and early '90s—when the emphasis on athletic prowess was beginning to change figure skating—Katarina's appearances reminded everyone that there was a lot more to her sport than landing a triple axel. She drove this point home in unforgettable fashion after gaining reinstatement for the 1994 Olympics in Lillehammer. Katarina, age 28, was a mature woman going up against a swarm of tiny teenagers. She skated a lovely final program that brought the crowd to its feet, and brought tears to many eyes. And although she finished seventh overall, she reaffirmed her place in the hearts of the sport's most ardent fans. To them, Kat will always be number one.

Acting lessons helped Katarina "become" the characters she portrayed in her programs

Kristi Yamaguchi

Five-year-old Kristi Yamaguchi was just like millions of other little girls in 1976, as she watched Dorothy Hamill win an Olympic gold medal: she was transfixed. Most of those little girls copied the figure skater's haircut. Kristi, however, decided to make figure skating her career. At first glance, she was not what you would consider an ideal candidate. Kristi had been born with severely pigeon-toed feet. For a good portion of her first two years, she wore casts to correct the problem. After that, she needed special shoes. Believing that skating would strengthen Kristi's legs, her parents agreed to support her skating ambitions.

Kristi entered her first competition when she was eight years old, and did well enough to convince experts that she could become a champion. Around this time she met her longtime coach, Christy Kjarsgaard. Within a year, the grind began. Kristi began setting her alarm for 4 A.M. so she could get a few hours on the ice each morning before school started. Her mother, Carole, would take her to practice. It was hard to imagine a child being so focused, but the older Kristi got, the more intensely she concentrated on achieving her goal. She wanted to do what Hamill had done, and she would make any sacrifice required to put herself in that position. "For a little kid," she says, "I worked incredibly hard."

In 1983, Kristi started skating with Rudy Galindo. At 4'6", Rudy was a small boy, so he needed a small partner. Kristi—who now stands just five feet tall and barely tips the scales at 100 pounds—was the perfect size. Thus began a long and productive on-ice relationship. In 1986, they

A favorite on both sides of the Pacific, Kristi was asked to participate in the opening festivities for the 1998 Olympics in Nagano, Japan.

Kristi's magnificent short program gave her a big lead going into the final skate at the 1992 Olympics in Albertville, France.

won the U.S. junior pairs competition. Meanwhile, Kristi was blossoming as a singles skater. In 1987, she won two international junior competitions. In 1988, Kristi won the World Junior Championship in both singles and pairs competition. She also got her picture in the back of *Sports Illustrated (SI),* in "Faces in the Crowd." Kristi was thrilled with the recognition, and began to think about getting her face out of the crowd and on to the cover.

In 1989, she won the U.S. pairs title with Galindo, and narrowly missed becoming the U.S. singles champion a couple of weeks later when she was edged out by Jill Trenary. As a second-place finisher, however, Kristi qualified for the World Championships. It marked the first time a U.S. woman had made the worlds in both singles and pairs since 1954! Kristi finished sixth in the singles and fifth with Galindo in the pairs. It was quite a showing.

Kristi decided she would try to make the 1992 Olympics in both singles and pairs. The demands of a dual career in figure skating are mind-boggling. Yet, in a sport where practicing is everything, Kristi was willing to practice twice as much as anyone else. "I knew it was difficult," she recalls, "but I really felt I could do it."

Sadly, Kristi's dream began to unravel in 1989. Her singles coach, Christy Kjarsgaard, married and moved to the Canadian city of

Edmonton. Kristi left her family so she could continue to train with her in Canada, and would fly back and forth in order to keep competing with Galindo. When her performance began to suffer from all the travel, however, the U.S. Figure Skating Association pressured her into making a choice. Kristi believed she had a better chance to win a gold medal going solo, but was reluctant to leave Galindo hanging. But when their pairs coach, Jim Hulick, died in December, she knew it was time to give up the dream. Galindo continued to train with Kristi—and the two won another U.S. title in 1990—but in 1991 they saw that their partnership would have to come to an end. "I figured we accomplished as much as we could together," Kristi recalls. "To improve in one or the other, I had to choose."

Meanwhile, Kristi was truly coming into her own as a singles skater. In 1990, she placed second in the U.S. Championships and won a gold medal at the Goodwill Games. In 1991, she won a silver medal at the nationals and then dazzled the sport by winning the World Championships in Munich. She finished ahead of two other talented Americans, Tonya Harding and Nancy Kerrigan. It was the first time one country had swept the top three spots in 73 years!

Kristi was peaking at just the right time. Smaller and more slender than her rivals, she brought unparalleled grace and artistry to the ice, and

Getting Personal

Kristi was born on July 12, 1971, in Hayward, California...A year before she got the skating bug, Kristi was enrolled in ballet classes. She continued to take dance classes while she skated, and claims this is what gave her an advantage when she reached the top levels of competition...After the 1976 Olympics, Kristi got a Dorothy Hamill doll and carried it with her everywhere for good luck...Her friends in California still call her by her old nickname: "Yama"...Her favorite TV shows are ER and Friends...In 1994, Kristi could have applied for reinstatement with the International Skating Union and competed in the Olympics. She chose not to. She had achieved her childhood dream, and did not want to tarnish it by trying for a second gold medal. Kristi admits that she was tempted to go for the gold medal in pairs, however...As part of the Stars on Ice tour, Kristi now skates in more than 50 programs a year.

Career Highlights

Year	Achievement
1988	World Junior Singles & Pairs Champion
1989	US Pairs Champion
1989	US Olympic Committee Figure Skating Athlete of the Year
1989	Olympic Festival Singles Champion
1990	US Pairs Champion
1991	World Singles Champion
1992	World Singles Champion
1992	Olympic Gold Medalist
1992	World Pro Champion
1994	World Pro Champion

rarely made even a miniscule mistake. Her specialty was the triple jump, which she could execute a number of ways. As the skating world began to prepare for the 1992 season, the only knock on Kristi was that she did not have the raw power needed to execute a triple axel. Harding could do it, and so could Japan's Midori Ito, but neither had Kristi's technical prowess.

Kristi put on an eye-popping performance at the nationals to win her first U.S. singles title, and came into the Olympics in Albertville, France, on an all-time high. During the short program, she displayed grace and athleticism in her routine, which included seven flawless triple jumps. As one writer put it, she skated "as if all that mattered was making people smile." Meanwhile, all the other women were so focused on out-jumping Ito and Harding that they all fell. Even Midori and Tonya fell trying to outdo each other! Two days later, Kristi performed her long routine. It was not as good, but it was good enough to win the gold. Just as she had dreamed four years earlier, her picture appeared on the cover of *SI*.

Kristi then moved on to the World Championships, which were being held near her home, in Oakland. Some thought she might have a letdown, but nothing could have been farther from the truth. Kristi was magnificent, and won her second world title in front of her family and all of her high school friends. No one had won the worlds twice in a row since Peggy Fleming in 1968.

After the World Championships, Kristi started thinking about the future. There was nothing left to prove at the amateur level; she had won everything in sight and finished first in 14 of her last 21 international competitions. In short, it was time to "cash in" on all those years of hard work.

Kristi decided to hit the road with the pro skating tour, where the physical demands on a skater are often tougher than in the amateur ranks. There are often several shows a week, and there is no sitting out with an ache or a sprain when 15,000 people have paid good money to watch you perform. Some skaters wither under this kind of schedule. Others fail to grow creatively and lose interest in the sport. But Kristi developed into a peerless performer and a real crowd-pleaser. "It's a tough schedule, but it lets you do what you want artistically and intellectually," she says of the Stars on Ice tour. Besides, she insists, "When you skate every night with the best entertainers on the ice, what could be greater?"

Off the ice, Kristi barely takes a breather. She is a spokeswoman for the 2002 Olympics in Salt Lake City and runs the Always Dream Foundation, which benefits underprivileged kids in northern California and Nevada. "It opened my eyes to develop this foundation," says Kristi, who hopes to take it nationwide. "You can never do enough to help."

Kristi's long program was a notch below her short program at the 1992 Olympics, but it was enough to win the gold medal.

What's Next

T here is a lot of debate concerning the current state of figure skating, and it involves people both on the inside of the sport and in the sports world in general. Is it fair, some ask, that the rules of competition so clearly favor young skaters? Those who want to see a change wonder if, in the name of technical achievement, an important part of the sport has been lost. There is perhaps no other competitive sport where athletes are considered "washed up" just as they hit what the rest of us would consider their physical primes. In skating, that has definitely become the case.

The trade-off is this: A skater in her twenties brings to the ice a special understanding of her craft, a maturity that comes through years of hard work and experience. But because of her more developed body, she is unlikely to be able to pull off the increasingly demanding moves that younger, smaller skaters can. It has nothing to do with athletic ability and everything to do with physics. Conversely, a 15-year-old can nail difficult jumps and string together combinations that would buckle the knees of an older skater. But can she really bring to a program the rich texture that an older skater can?

The "pro-youth" people say yes, simply look at Oksana Baiul and Tara Lipinski. Their opponents, however, would argue that these days what passes for artistry is simply programmed into girls at the same time they are learning their triple lutzes.

Two things weigh against the argument that the sport is becoming too young. First, the assumption that figure skating must follow the same rules as other sports is wrong. For better or worse, skating has never been like other sports. Why should it start now?

Second, there are profound financial considerations involved. It costs a family a lot of money to support a daughter's skating ambitions, and frequently the results are ruinous. A mother and father would be far more likely to make that immense commitment of time and money if they knew a concrete picture of their daughter's future might emerge by the time she reaches 11 or 12. That can only be good for skating, because it means that more families will take this chance, and thus more raw talent will be fed into the system.

On the other end of the equation, the "younger is better" position also benefits skating by feeding more proven champions into the professional ranks while they are still young. With the rare exception of someone like Katarina Witt, a skater turning pro in her twenties usually has only a few years on tour before the grind of 50 or more shows a season forces her to quit. Theoretically, at least, turning pro as a teenager guarantees a few more prime years on tour. And again, this can only be good for skating, for it raises the overall quality of what the public sees.

Assuming no dramatic changes are in the offing, what lies ahead in the world of competitive skating is an increased focus on mid-air acrobatics. A handful of today's skaters are already attempting things like quadruple jumps and somersaults, and stringing together unprecedented combinations. Meanwhile, coaches are exploring ways to push the existing limits right to the edge, and keeping their eyes peeled for a skater with groundbreaking potential.

Nothing is ever a given in sports, but as skating enters the 21st century, there is one thing fans can count on. With television ratings and ticket sales to events higher than ever, skating has established a niche in the world of competitive sports that will not be diminished. Finally, the women who take the ice are being recognized for a lot more than their femininity. They may be young, and they may be pretty, but figure skaters are no longer "athletes in disguise."

INDEX

PAGE NUMBERS IN ITALICS REFER TO ILLUSTRATIONS.